HAMLET *Observed*

The National Theatre at Work

Jonathan Croall

The Author

Jonathan Croall worked as an editor in book publishing and newspapers before becoming a writer and journalist. His previous books include a biography of A.S. Neill, an oral history of the Second World War, and a children's novel. He has directed and written plays for the London fringe, and now specialises in writing about theatre.

He is the editor of two magazines published by the National Theatre, *StageWrite* and *Ensemble*. His most recent book is *Gielgud: A Theatrical Life*.

Hamlet Observed is published by
NT Publications
Royal National Theatre
South Bank, London SE1 9PX
www.nationaltheatre.org.uk

Editor Lyn Haill

Designed by Stephen Cummiskey

Cover photograph of Simon Russell Beale by Clare Park, designed for the NT poster by Michael Mayhew

Rehearsal and production photographs by Catherine Ashmore

Typeset in Ehrhardt

Printed by Battley Brothers, Clapham, London SW4 0JN

ISBN No. 0 9519943 4 4

This book is published with the help of a grant from

The Royal National Theatre Foundation

The Royal National Theatre Foundation is a registered charity, independent of the Royal National Theatre. It has two purposes. One is to help past and present members of the National's staff and company who are in need. For example, it has helped to pay special medical expenses, has made grants in cases of exceptional personal distress, and has assisted in the completion of education and training. The second purpose is to help meet the cost of special projects which would otherwise be beyond the scope of the National's normal budgets.

The Foundation relies on charitable donations. If you would like to help this cause, please send a donation to The Treasurer, Royal National Theatre Foundation, Upper Ground, London SE1 9PX.

Registered Charity 271706

Introduction

John Caird's production of *Hamlet,* which opened in the Lyttelton theatre in September 2000, was the fourth to be staged by the National Theatre. The first in 1963, starring Peter O'Toole and directed by Laurence Olivier, was the opening performance at the National's temporary home at the Old Vic. In 1976 Peter Hall's production, starring Albert Finney, officially opened the Lyttelton theatre. Thirteen years later Richard Eyre directed the play in the Olivier with Daniel Day-Lewis as Hamlet, the part later being taken over by Ian Charleson.

Simon Russell Beale's millennium Hamlet has been acclaimed as one of the finest of recent times. I was fortunate enough to witness at close quarters the process by which he created the role. Thanks to the generosity and trust of John Caird and his actors, who allowed me unique access to their act of creation, I was able to sit in on rehearsals, observe them at work behind the scenes, and follow their progress on tour, most notably in the historic setting of Elsinore in Denmark. Throughout this time I was able to talk freely with the actors, director, designer, the stage management team, and others.

This book is not intended to be an exhaustive account of the entire production. It is rather a snapshot of key moments in the making of *Hamlet,* intermingled with the day-to-day ideas, opinions, hopes and fears of those involved. I hope that what for me was an immensely stimulating and absorbing experience has resulted in a true picture of how the National moved one of the most challenging plays in the repertoire from page to stage.

Contents

Photographs between pages 42 and 59

The Cast

Hamlet

by **William Shakespeare**

Horatio	**Simon Day**
Hamlet, *Prince of Denmark*	**Simon Russell Beale**
Hamlet, *his father*	**Sylvester Morand**
Claudius, *his uncle*	**Peter McEnery**
Gertrude, *his mother*	**Sara Kestelman**
Polonius, *Lord Chamberlain*	**Denis Quilley**
Laertes, *his son*	**Guy Lankester**
Ophelia, *his daughter*	**Cathryn Bradshaw**
Reynaldo, *his servant*	**Edward Gower**
Rosencrantz	**Christopher Staines**
Guildenstern	**Paul Bazely**
Player King	**Sylvester Morand**
Player Queen	**Janet Spencer-Turner**
Other Players	**Chloe Angharad**
	Michael Wildman
Francisco, *a soldier*	**Edward Gower**
Barnardo, *an officer*	**Ken Oxtoby**
Marcellus, *an officer*	**Martin Chamberlain**
Osric, *a courtier*	**Michael Wildman**
Gentlewomen	**Chloe Angharad**
	Janet Spencer-Turner
The Grave-digger	**Denis Quilley**
The Priest	**Ken Oxtoby**

Music played by **Jonathan Cooper** (Music Director/keyboards), **Rebecca Brown**
(viola/recorder), **Belinda Sykes/Ann Allen** (oboe/shawm/recorder)

Director	**John Caird**
Designer	**Tim Hatley**
Lighting Designer	**Paul Pyant**
Music	**John Cameron**
Fight Director	**Terry King**
Sound Designer	**Christopher Shutt**
Company Voice Work	**Patsy Rodenburg**

Staff Director
Stephen Wrentmore

Production Manager
Mark Dakin

Stage Manager
Trish Montemuro

Deputy Stage Manager
Fiona Bardsley

Assistant Stage Managers
Valerie Fox, Andrew Speed

Assistant to the Designer
Stuart D Nunn

Assistant to the Lighting Designer
Pete Bull

Assistant Voice Coach
Jeannette Nelson

Deputy Production Manager (*Hamlet*)
Annie Eves-Boland

Assistant Production Manager
Paul Atkinson

Costume Supervisor
Carrie Bayliss
assisted by **Deborah Norman**

Production Photographer
Catherine Ashmore

First performances in the Lyttelton Theatre from 15 July 2000,
before visiting Festival Theatre, Malvern 2-12 August, Kronborg Castle,
Elsinore, Denmark 16-24 August.

Hamlet then opened at the Royal National Theatre's Lyttelton Theatre on
5 September 2000, before visiting Theatre Royal, Brighton; Theatre Royal, Glasgow;
Gaiety Theatre, Dublin; Stadsteatern, Stockholm, Sweden; National Theatre,
Belgrade, Federal Republic of Yugoslavia; Theatre Royal, Plymouth; Theatre Royal,
Bath; His Majesty's Theatre, Aberdeen; and the United States.

Opening in the National's Olivier Theatre: June 2001

The production was sponsored by KPMG

1.   *The Beginnings*

T he idea of staging a new production of *Hamlet* emerged in the early summer of 1999. Trevor Nunn, who had become director of the National in 1997, had broken with recent tradition by creating an ensemble of actors, who were to perform six works in repertory during that year. One of the plays chosen was *Money*, a rarely performed Victorian 'serious comedy' by Edward Bulwer-Lytton, to be directed by John Caird and starring Simon Russell Beale.

John Caird 'Lytton's hero, Alfred Evelyn, is a kind of cross between Hamlet and himself. In the play he frequently breaks into soliloquy mode, and muses on the relationship between man and money. One of his speeches was so Hamlet-like that within days of starting rehearsals I thought, This is ridiculous, why has Simon never played Hamlet? Here he was working on a part he could do in his sleep; we had been using a Rolls-Royce to get to the corner shop. By the time we got to the technicals it was clear to me that he was going to be a triumph as Evelyn. So I said to him, This is clearly a sketch for our production of *Hamlet*: why don't we do the real thing? He bit immediately.'

Now thirty-nine, Simon had been wanting to play Hamlet for many years, and had got near to doing so more than once. Tentative plans for Sam Mendes to direct him in the part had been recently revived, the production to be staged at the Donmar Warehouse. However, when it became clear that the film *American Beauty* was going to send Mendes' career into orbit, he agreed Simon should go ahead without him. John Caird therefore approached Trevor Nunn, who immediately offered to stage his production of *Hamlet* with Simon at the National. It was also decided that the play should tour in the UK and Europe, and possibly in America.

Simon Russell Beale 'It seemed to me a wonderful idea, because John is one of the most collaborative directors I know, if not the most. As I was aware from working with him on *Money* and *Candide*, he's incredibly open and generous to other people's ideas, which is a very great strength. I think we worked well together because we complemented each other: I'm obsessed with the logic of story-telling. He is too, but much freer, and much more aware of what's beautiful to look at. Intellectually he's very impressive, yet not too heavy. He's also very funny: I thought there would probably be more laughs than usual in a *Hamlet* that he was directing.'

Although both Olivier and Hall had done the longest possible version, which normally runs for around four and a half hours, John followed more recent directors in deciding to cut the play substantially. In doing so he knew he wanted to lose the political background, much of which he felt Shakespeare may have added at a later stage. As well as making many major cuts in advance, he chose to do the detailed cutting in collaboration with the actors at the beginning of rehearsals.

One of his early intentions was to emphasise the play's religious elements. This idea informed his initial discussions with the designer Tim Hatley, who had worked with him at the National on his production of Pam Gems' *Stanley*.

Tim Hatley 'Having talked at length with John about the play, my aim was to create a design that made Elsinore both a prison and a religious place, but also flexible for the actors. My original design was a big ruined cathedral, with corridors and tunnels and levels, a banqueting table, lots of icons, and chandeliers inspired by the reference to "this majestical roof fretted with golden fire". But this proved too expensive, and not very practical for touring. So we started again, and stripped everything down to the minimum.'

Left with just a floor and three walls, John wanted a design that would reflect a more metaphorical look at the play, something that would get away from architecture and focus on the idea of journeys, of which there are so many in *Hamlet*. He was also playing with the idea of the company becoming a group of strolling players, or maybe ghosts, re-enacting the tragedy of *Hamlet*. This notion inspired the final design, a set consisting solely of the chandeliers, and a collection of trunks that the actors would bring on, rearrange or take off the stage as required.

Because of the delay caused by the need to re-design the set, the lighting designer Paul Pyant was not able to see it until the first production meeting. By then John was already working with the composer and orchestrator John Cameron, whose brief was not only to find suitable existing music, but also to create new material.

John Cameron 'Several months before rehearsals began we started to talk about a suitable musical language for the play. We tried to think of the music as being like a lighting cue, as part of the flavour of the piece rather than an add-on feature. John gave me pointers to where it might be needed, and I eventually came back with a load of unaccompanied motets, which seemed to convey the right spiritual feeling we were looking for.'

Finding the right actors for the principal parts was straightforward in some cases, less so in others. John preferred not to cast according to physical type, as was evident in his decision to work with Simon, whose short, stocky physique flew in the face of the received wisdom about Hamlet's looks. For John this was irrelevant. 'Simon is wonderfully equipped for the part. He's a man of extreme intelligence, of great complexity emotionally, and fantastic humour. That's what his Hamlet is going to be like.'

In casting Claudius he wanted to get away from the conventional notion of the hard-drinking, swaggering, big 'bloat' king, and to create a more subtle character. To this end he chose Peter McEnery, who had played both Laertes and Hamlet in earlier productions. 'I felt Peter would be perfect as a plausible, complicated machiavellian villain, who was also a sexy and attractive younger brother, someone who could have turned Gertrude's head at a time of great grief. He's an intelligent man with great feeling, capable as an actor of combining a glamorous exterior with a steely interior. I loved the thought of the wry and ironic delivery he would bring to Claudius.'

As Gertrude he cast Sara Kestelman, an experienced Shakespearean actress who had previously played Goneril and Lady Macbeth for the RSC. 'I've so often seen Gertrude played as the once-beautiful flibberty-gibbet who regrets her looks are going. I felt it was essential to have a Gertrude who was mighty, someone who was capable of Greek-tragedy size of feeling, because I knew Simon would be doing that. Sara is an emotional and vulnerable woman, who as an actress has instant access to the complexities of her own character, and can turn them on brilliantly. Gertrude is a small part when measured by the number of her lines, but a large part for the amount of time she's on the stage. You need an actress who can bring an awful lot to it that isn't in the text. Sara has an ability to fill a silence with a look or a gesture, the great gift of making an unspoken moment eloquent.'

The choice of Polonius was made for him. Denis Quilley, who had doubled as Claudius and the Ghost in Peter Hall's production, was now a member of the ensemble at the National, with a leading part in *Money*. 'As Denis was leaving the first-night party he said to me, "I'll do a Polonius for you if you like." I said, "You're on." It was that simple. I wanted a Polonius who was neither a doddery old fool nor simply a nasty, evil politician, but a complex human being. I knew that Denis, one of the finest Shakespearean actors of his generation, would give me that. He's also one of the great comedians, capable of being brilliantly and effortlessly funny without ever being crude or cheap. This made him a perfect choice for the Gravedigger once I'd decided to double up parts in a smaller ensemble.'

In casting Ophelia he settled on Cathryn Bradshaw, who had played the part ten years before in a Cheek by Jowl production. 'The central thing about the relationship between Hamlet and Ophelia is that they understand each other. She's not as emotionally complicated as him, but she has the same sense of morality and goodness. Cathryn is an instinctive actress, and emotionally accessible and vulnerable in all the right ways for the part. You've got to have someone who understands the importance of spirituality in Ophelia, and she has that kind of imagination. I thought she would make a suitable emotional twin for Simon. One has to be able to believe that when Hamlet returns from Wittenberg for his father's funeral, she will be the first person he will turn to in his grief, and that from that moment until his first line in the play there's been a close relationship between them of friendship and love.'

Having taken on Sylvester Morand for the Ghost and Simon Day for Laertes, John still had no Horatio. 'The part is rather mysterious and without clear character or age delineations. The only important stipulation is that he should be a genuine friend of Hamlet. At the same time, as I began to see Horatio as the storyteller of the play, he was becoming increasingly important. It became apparent that we needed someone who was completely au fait with Simon, who enjoyed working with me, and who would have an instinctive sympathy for the ideas I was proposing. Simon Day had been a member of the National's ensemble, and worked with me in both *Money* and *Candide*. The minute I had the idea of moving him from Laertes to Horatio, I knew I had the right answer.' Once this was done, he could bring in Guy Lankester, an actor he considered a perfect Laertes.

John consulted Simon about all the main casting decisions. 'With major parts it's always wise to check that there isn't a history of difficulties that might cause a problem. Simon is an extremely generous actor who finds it very difficult not to have something nice to say about somebody, whatever his experience of them. Very occasionally he will voice a negative opinion about an actor, but that's usually because they've behaved extremely badly or cruelly to another actor. But having given his opinion he'd say, It's up to you.'

Contrary to his normal way of approaching a part, Simon began to learn Hamlet's lines well in advance. Two months before rehearsals began he and John started to meet once a week. At each session they read an act together, discussed the set, and John's concept for the production. They agreed that the play was essentially about a group of people who all loved or wanted to love each other, but whose love was destroyed by circumstances. It was here that other important ideas used in the production emerged, including the central one of having Horatio act as the storyteller, and the character who starts and ends the play.

These fruitful preliminary sessions had an extra dimension because, by a sad coincidence, both John's and Simon's mothers had died shortly before they started to meet. Before rehearsals began Simon was asked to give a lecture on *Hamlet* at Stratford. 'My first response was that I wouldn't have anything to say until we'd started to work on the play. But writing it actually sorted out a lot of my ideas. The most important personal one was the death of my mother. She was an extraordinary woman, and my relationship with her was a very close and loving one. I felt it would be a privilege to be able, with her, to explore the greatest meditations on grief and death ever written, and that my performance would be a kind of tribute to her.'

2.   *The Rehearsals*

Monday 22 May   R ehearsal Room 2, the National Theatre. Morning.
The company has assembled for the first day of
rehearsals. After being greeted by Trevor Nunn and introduced to the National's
heads of department, the actors settle round a makeshift square of tables, armed
with their Arden editions of the play. John Caird sets out his ideas.

'The most significant and tricky thing about directing *Hamlet* is that it's both an
intensely naturalistic drama and an extraordinary piece of metaphysical poetry
and philosophy. Sometimes the two run in parallel, and sometimes they defeat
each other if you're not taking into account the difference between them. A good
production needs to supply both of those elements to an audience.

'Of all Shakespeare's plays, *Hamlet* is the one which most profoundly examines
the nature of mankind, in a world where people reflect deeply about themselves.
It's a portrait of the life and death of an unbelievably complex man: all
Shakespeare's most fascinating thoughts are there in Hamlet's mind. It seems to
me a deeply autobiographical play; you can almost hear him as he's writing, not
caring where he takes the play, being driven by his thoughts rather than by the
plot.'

He outlines a few problems and questions, and some tentative solutions:

◆ *Hamlet* is textually the most complex of all Shakespeare's works. It went
through more changes than any other of his plays, and is a curious mixture
of styles. To play a full version, using all the available material, is to shirk
the responsibility to make the evening coherent.

◆ Part of it is a history play, but a rotten one: the history is boring, it doesn't
work dramatically. Fortinbras seems not to be part of the original version.
The Danish politics could be dropped.

◆ The play is ostensibly set in medieval Denmark, but actually it's an
Elizabethan Denmark. So it's really a mythological place. The time is now,
whenever now is.

♦ The story is about real people and real relationships. But it also has a ghost with a personality, who is not a figment of Hamlet's imagination. How do you deal with the supernatural element?

♦ The society is one that believes in God; Hamlet's thoughts are pre-enlightenment. So the production must be suffused with religious certainty. If you set it after the seventeenth century an audience loses patience with the religious arguments.

♦ How do you physicalise the metaphysical? The production needs a set that allows all the imagery about heaven and earth to be liberated, one that reflects the extraordinary beauty of the form, line and imagery of the play. The solution is to have one that doesn't require conventional scenery.

Tim Hatley then shows the company the set model, its floor littered with trunks, and its ceiling hung with numerous lamps that can be individually lowered to any level. The back wall of the set opens a chink to let people in from the world outside Elsinore. The actors comment approvingly on the set's beauty and simplicity.

Tim then reveals his provisional thoughts about costume. He's aiming for a mixture of period and modern, clothes that will emphasise the dark, ecclesiastical tone of the production. 'Maybe Danish Renaissance sludge, with gold for the royal characters,' he says. He's been looking at Eastern fabrics, and also Renaissance paintings for the dark, rich colours he wants to achieve.

During the lunch break news gets round of the death of one of the great Hamlets, John Gielgud. Denis Quilley, who worked with him at the National, recalls his powerful rendering of Hamlet's 'Oh what a rogue and peasant slave' soliloquy at a gala celebration on the National's last night at the Old Vic.

The actors start to read the play. This is no ordinary readthrough: having accepted in principle John's idea of losing about an hour's running time from the play, they begin the collective cutting exercise. 'I think we should cut early and stick to it,' John says. 'We need to be bold, look out for scenes that overstay their welcome, or speeches that just go on too long.'

The radical intentions are clear from the start, the first scene being cut ruthlessly from 180 to 50 lines. Gone is the exchange between Marcellus and Horatio on the political background, and the conflict with Norway. Throughout the afternoon the actors seem more than willing to lose lines, and sometimes substantial speeches, for the greater good of the production.

The constant cutting means many interruptions, during which John and the actors share some first thoughts about the characters. At moments the session seems more like a university seminar than a rehearsal: there's a learned discussion about why Hamlet is studying theology at Wittenberg. But already some of the motivation is being teased out. Why, it's asked, does Claudius want initially to keep Hamlet in Denmark? 'He didn't want to just kill his brother, he wanted to *be* him,' John suggests. 'So nothing must change, he needs Hamlet to be his son.'

The attention to detail and the skill of the cutting are impressive, as is John's breadth of knowledge. The actual reading is downbeat, almost throwaway; emotions are being kept well in check. But there's already an arresting quality about Simon's reading of Hamlet, and his speaking of the verse. His first soliloquy, 'O that this too too sullied flesh would melt', is clear, unflashy and intelligent.

At this rate the readthrough seems likely to last for a couple of weeks. Surely the actors will want to be on their feet well before then?

▼ ▼ ▼

Simon Russell Beale 'Hamlet is so extraordinary, and yet there's an everyman quality about him. So he's really what you want to make of him. I haven't any game plan, because I don't think the part demands that. It's more a question of looking down into yourself, which makes it difficult.

'I flatter myself that the wit will be all right, and the wryness and the self-deprecation. I know I'd quite like him to be funny, but I don't quite know how I'm going to achieve that. I know I have a weakness to be vocally over-elaborate, but the really difficult bit will be controlling the huge waves of emotion. I don't want to indulge in sobbing too often, so it's a question of finding the right moments for the distress to show, such as perhaps the Yorick speech or the closet scene.

'I was worried about the madness, whether I might have to do something extraordinary like stand on my head. I'm not very good at tricks or inventing bits of business, I'm not the type. In any case, for all his intelligence there's something very innocent about Hamlet, which I think is probably best served by not trying to be too clever with him. So I suspect my interpretation will be quite simple in the end.'

John Caird 'I work in a way that requires people to study the play together, to say what they think. There's no hierarchy of opinion: from the most senior actor to the most junior member of stage management, if people have an idea I like them to voice it. Some ideas are excellent and ought to be used, but even if it's a bad idea, it's all the better for being voiced, because it might start a good one, or put to bed some bad ones that are fomenting in other people's minds. One should never mock a bad idea, one should always think about it, and explain why it's not going to work.

'If you have everybody able to voice their opinion, they slowly become a company, they pull together well, they become equal partners in the sharing of the play's message. In this way you lose any sense of hierarchy, or of subversion or bitterness or disappointment – which is often an artist's life just under the skin.'

Tuesday 30 May
Rehearsal room. Afternoon. It's Day 6, the company are up to Act 4, and still cutting. 'It's important to keep the story active, so that the only things we hear about are new things,' John says. Scene four, Hamlet's meeting with Fortinbras' army, disappears, and with it the entire soliloquy 'How all occasions do inform against me'. Simon is relaxed about this decision: 'I've got too much to say anyway.' Sometimes single lines or even half lines within a speech are dropped, though care is taken to preserve the iambic pentameter.

There's a discussion about the drowning of Ophelia, whether Gertrude actually witnessed it, and if so why she didn't try to save her. John believes there's a reason why Shakespeare gave the speech to the queen rather than have the story told by a shepherd or a waiting woman. 'There's evidence that he wanted us to be mourning two women at the same time,' he suggests.

On to Act 5, and the graveyard scene. Hamlet's musings on lawyers ('Where be his quiddities now?') has to go. Here the question of Hamlet's age comes up. Simon: 'I know he's thirty, but couldn't we make it thirty-nine?' John: 'If Denmark is a state of mind, so too is Hamlet's age.' Simon: 'And his weight?'

The more obviously tedious lines or speeches are met with groans or giggles. John greets the penultimate scene with horror: 'Another killer! The whole thing is a rewrite.' The necessary lines are cut, after which the company reads it again. 'It never makes sense in the theatre, but now it does,' John says. The session ends with a debate about Hamlet's state of mind in the 'Not a whit' speech: how reconciled is he to the idea of death?

Tomorrow will see the end of the cutting exercise. On Thursday the actors will get the resulting script, and read the play straight through.

▼ ▼ ▼

John Caird 'I've always felt that Ophelia and Gertrude are deeply connected emotionally, and that was why Shakespeare has Gertrude bringing the news of Ophelia's death. The play fools around a lot with the concept of time and generations, and in a way they are the same women, they have a similar relationship to the men in the play. Gertrude is the present queen, and Ophelia would have been the new queen, and they would both have been married to a man called Hamlet. In many ways Hamlet is his father made young, so it's almost as if Gertrude is watching what happened to her when she was a young woman. These connections are in the text just waiting for you to discover them.'

Sara Kestelman 'I've thought a lot about the nature of Gertrude's relationship with Claudius. Were they having an affair or not? Was it a one-night fling that suddenly blossomed into something else? Was it something they had been nursing for years from a distance? How bad was the marriage with old Hamlet? Was it arranged, a marriage they had to suffer?

'I've asked myself some basic questions about her by examining the text just from her point of view. The more I did so, the more I saw her as enormously courageous. She's rightfully a queen, and is able to inhabit the world of the men and find her place naturally in it. Apart from the closet scene, which has a real emotional and inexorable dynamic, her part is very spare. But I don't think her lack of words weakens her.'

Cathryn Bradshaw 'With Ophelia you have to do a lot of detective work, as the part is underwritten. One thing I didn't want to do was to present her as a victim from the very first moment. Ophelia is often seen as passive throughout, but I want to get away from that. My idea is to show a fairly happy woman, blossoming from being in love: for a fleeting moment she has all her hopes ahead of her, and then slowly she disintegrates.'

Monday 5 June

Rehearsal room. Late afternoon. The session has ended, and most of the actors have left. At the side of the stage area the stage manager Trish Montemuro is sorting out the schedule for the week's rehearsals, while her assistants Andrew Speed and Valerie Fox are busy clearing away the trunks.

Near the back wall Simon and Guy Lankester, playing Laertes, are rehearsing the duel with the fight director Terry King. It's still early days, and they work gingerly through the first two sequences of the fight. Simon, who seems anxious as they parry and thrust, is surprisingly quick and light on his feet for someone of his build.

▼ ▼ ▼

Trish Montemuro 'We try to create a conducive environment for rehearsals, but every production is different. With this one we've had a huge input into what's been going on onstage, because John has left all the box-changing to us. If he wants something to be created for a scene, he says what its central architecture is – a clifftop, Polonius' desk – and we work out how to do it. With a really complicated change we ask him for help. For the quayside scene, for example, he had the idea that Rosenscrantz and Guildernstern would climb over the hilltop, so that all eyes would be drawn to them, and away from the box-shifting.

'To supplement the stage crew, we have the actors moving the trunks, with the help of Andrew and Val, who will be in costume. It's known as Pickfords, and the actors get paid a few pounds extra for doing it. But it doesn't come naturally to everyone, so it will be up to us to watch every scene change very carefully.

Simon Russell Beale 'Before I started I was very worried about the question of Hamlet's madness. But now it's all become much clearer. He's not mad, but the pressure he's under makes him think he might be. If people around you start saying you're losing your marbles, of course you begin to worry about it. I think he's just slightly off-kilter, but for a perfectly normal and understandable reason, which is his grief at discovering that his stepfather has killed his father, and that his mother has married a murderer.

Thursday 8 June

Rehearsal room. Morning. The cutting is over, the exercise has produced a script that, read without interruption or pause, is just over two hours long. The actors are now on their feet, and blocking the moves for the long second scene in Act 2. The room is full of trunks.

The atmosphere is relaxed and jokey, but purposeful. Simon and Denis work on Polonius' meeting with Hamlet as he reads ('Words, words, words'). In place of the usual mockery of Polonius, John wants to introduce an element of danger, even a hint that Hamlet might kill Polonius. At once the scene takes on a different edge. When it comes to Hamlet's soliloquy 'What a piece of work is a man', Simon starts to put light and shade into the speech, conveying both intelligence and world-weariness. Unlike most of the company, he's already off the book.

When they reach the entry of the Players, with Sylvester Morand doubling the Player King with the Ghost, John observes: 'This is where a crack opens in the play, and new characters come in from another dimension, from the real world. Maybe we need a touch of music here? It's a Pirandellian moment. We need to find a magical way of Hamlet meeting the Players.' The Players sit on the trunks for a few minutes, discussing Hamlet's keen interest in the theatre, and how it might be used.

The 'pastoral-comical' speech is then explored. Denis plays it as Polonius showing off to those around him, which works well; the tricky part is to choreograph the rising laughter from Hamlet, Rosencrantz and Guildernstern. Eventually they get there.

Later, for the Player King's Hecuba speech, John suggests that Hamlet, with his passion for the theatre, might decide to mime the early part, sword in hand. Mesmerised by this suggestion, Simon becomes intense, enjoying the melodrama – but then wonders if the idea isn't a bit heavy-handed. It's decided to leave it in for the moment.

At the end of the session the costumes are wheeled in on a dress rail. 'Let's do it

with just a rail and a skip', says John, who minutes before has refused to be drawn
into discussions about possible cuts to the design budget.

▼ ▼ ▼

Denis Quilley 'Polonius is a difficult character. You have a feeling, as Harley
  Granville Barker says in his *Preface*, that Shakespeare changed his mind
  about him halfway through: he starts with his wise advice to his son, and
  then you get this silly stuff. So he's often played simply as an old buffer, and
  for all the comic mileage that can be got out of him.

  'Both John and I think that's wrong, so we're taking the opposite approach,
  and going for the reality. If you look at his lines, for example in his scene
  with Ophelia, and forget how you've seen it done before, they're the words
  of a very intelligent man and a very loving father, who has a deep concern
  for his daughter. He's conceited and a bit of a bore, but extremely intelligent
  and powerful. He's the kind of guy who would stand up at the bar in the
  Garrick Club and tell long, boring stories that he thinks are funny, but
  which aren't.

  'But that doesn't make him any less formidable. He's the king's right-hand
  man, so he's not an idiot; in fact he's a consummate manipulator, a real
  diplomatic fixer who manipulates Claudius.'

Peter McEnery 'I think Shakespeare wrote Claudius as an out-and-out villain,
  and I've often seen him played as that from his first entrance. But I'm more
  interested in the denial in his character, in the fact that he doesn't want to
  face his crime, and his guilty conscience about it. As we're emphasising the
  religious aspect of the play, John suggested you could see Claudius not just
  as the king but also as the chief priest. That's been very helpful to me, it
  gives him an austerity, it's made it easier to avoid the obvious, moustache-
  twirling villain.'

Wednesday 14 June

Rehearsal room. Afternoon. The blocking has reached the graveyard scene. John
has decided that the second character at the start of the scene is not another
gravedigger, as he is often played, but the tiresome courtier Osric, played by
Michael Wildman. This seems to fit with the officiousness of the character.
Simon Day wonders if Horatio knows of Ophelia's death and imminent funeral,

and has brought Hamlet there on purpose. Or does he want to stop him going into the graveyard? They experiment with alternative versions, including Horatio only meeting Hamlet by chance at the graveyard.

Denis is playing the Gravedigger as an ex-army rather than a rustic type. There's a brief debate about the kind of man he is. John sees him as uneducated but intelligent, in contrast to 'the educated Hooray Henry' that is Osric. 'When Hamlet the aristocrat arrives he has a real rapport with him,' he suggests. They look at ways of highlighting this rapport.

They come to 'Alas, poor Yorick', which Simon delivers with effective sadness. Denis wonders if the Gravedigger could belatedly realise who Hamlet is? Though there's no hint of this in the text, it's seen as a good idea, and a bit of business is inserted: a raised eyebrow to Horatio, a nod, and the Gravedigger doffs his cap.

Another inventive stroke from John is to convert Hamlet's four rhymed lines 'Imperious Caesar etc' into a song, begun by Denis and taken up in harmony by Simon. Both actors have excellent singing voices, and allied with some inventive comic business with the skull it works a treat.

The day ends with the actors trying to choreograph the difficult moment when Laertes, played by Guy Lankester, and Hamlet both jump into Ophelia's grave, and have to be restrained.

▼ ▼ ▼

Guy Lankester 'Laertes is a difficult part to play, because you disappear for such a long time. By the time you come back a lot of the story has been told, and you then have three scenes each with a major speech, which you have to do at top pitch in response to your father's death, your sister's madness and then her death. With each of them there's very little time to build up to anything, and no real time for discovery.'

Simon Day 'I think you have to play Horatio straight down the line, as a very generous, unselfish man, who doesn't really have an attitude to things unless it reflects Hamlet's reaction. He's a support for Hamlet, but not a sounding board, he never offers him advice. He's just there so Hamlet can think that there's someone out there in the world who is good, that despite all the shit that's going on and people's dodgy moral frameworks, there's still Horatio.'

Monday 19 June
After four weeks the company is half way through the rehearsal period. With the cutting and blocking completed, the actors are starting to come off the book. Some of them are also beginning to have short sessions with the staff director Stephen Wrentmore, who is working on the kind of detail there's no time to go into during the main rehearsals. John is pleased with progress so far.

▼ ▼ ▼

John Caird 'I think we're very much on course. The actors are beginning to be in control of the words, they're starting to increase the tension, but still doing a great deal of refining. We've had no major problems. There have been some difficulties of interpretation, but nothing that hasn't been amicably sorted out through discussion.

'One of my jobs is to persuade the actors to be compelled by the choices I've made, otherwise you get no unity. I think they've been given plenty of opportunity for their own invention, even if there's no real room for fundamental differences of interpretation or opinion. But together we've discovered things in the text that we didn't realise were there, which have surprised me as much as anyone else.

'My concept has been easier to put into practice than I thought it would be. The success of a production that relies on the metaphorical use of objects is always difficult to estimate until you get started. But this one has yielded very well, because it's so adaptable. With this kind of set you're not tied to anything, it's all so easy. At any moment you can say, Let's have a completely bare stage, or, You need such and such a prop, why don't you use a box. You don't have to say, We'll bring a cupboard in, or, We haven't got a chair. The literal way is such a curb to the imagination.

'I really am inventing it as I go along. I think it through with each scene, because that way you get a pure sense of what is necessary. If you work it out on paper without the actors there, often it just seems stale and intractable in practice. It's a high-risk method, but it's the only way to do it, to wait until you're in the company of all the different intelligences you're working with, and then let it come out of the imagination.

'I talk to the actors quite a lot about what a line means, but I never tell them how to say it. If you take a moment where you think a character is angry or grief-struck, there are fifty ways of showing that. If you try and lead an actor into the way you would do it yourself, you're simply limiting their mode of expression. You have to give them the what and the why, but never the how. They know much better than you how to do it: that's what makes them good actors.

'If you have an open relationship with the actors you'll get plenty of surprises. But you have to be receptive to atmosphere and vigilant to spot the good stuff coming from them. You can analyse a character as much as you like beforehand, but you won't get much out of it until an actor plays it. Then the magical chemistry happens, the combination of the actor's personality and the written role gives it the absolute reality that Shakespeare intended, but could never exactly prophesy because he didn't know the actors. That's the great genius of his work, it allows so many different types of actor to play the same role successfully.'

Simon Russell Beale 'I'm beginning to sniff the shape of the part now. The more I explore it, the more I think Hamlet is an innocent abroad. He's fantastically clever, but completely inexperienced. I'm sure that's why Shakespeare makes him a student at Wittenberg; you don't send a crown prince off to university unless you're deliberately saying something. He certainly has no experience of the real world, and he's not at all a political animal.

'I still haven't decided whether it's the chip of ice in the heart, and that Hamlet's problem is that he can't breathe. You could spend so much of the time sobbing, and I don't want to do that; I think his problem is deeper and colder than that. I'm trying not to have too many moments of crisis. But I have found one where I want the distress to happen, and that's the Yorick scene. Here was someone Hamlet loved, so it must be devastating for him to be suddenly holding his skull. Talking about death in the abstract is all well and good, but this is the first time he has actually seen the physical degradation.

'I don't want to force the emotion, I need to get there a little bit more slowly. The next weeks are going to be the interesting ones, because what we have been doing up to now has all been quite technical, and we've been able to do the gags. But from here on the challenge will be to get the emotional arc right.'

Peter McEnery 'A lot of Claudius' part has been cut, notably his long scene with Laertes, which is fine. Those two weeks spent cutting were very valuable. What often happens is that when you run the production you find that it's too long, so you start dishing out cuts. That's very disconcerting, it throws everybody, and upsets the rhythm. But going through the text with a toothcomb and getting everyone's agreement about the cuts has prevented anything like that. Of course you keep an ear open all the time in case a line needs to go back, and that's happened now and then.'

Cathryn Bradshaw 'John's explanation at the beginning was so scholarly it had me worried. But when it comes to his directing, all that intellectual stuff stops, and something much more organic takes over. He really lets us fly, but he'll also tell us if something isn't working. For instance he slightly toned down my exasperation with Polonius in the first scene, but I was still able to keep that feeling within me. He doesn't disturb you on the path you're on, he just shows you another way.'

Stephen Wrentmore 'It's been a remarkably happy production so far. The period when you're cutting the play is usually the most fraught, because people are counting the number of lines they've lost. This time they were offering to have lines cut. That spirit has continued all through.'

Sara Kestelman 'During rehearsals we've been able to say whatever we've wanted to say. As a result everyone feels engaged. As a director John is absolutely at the helm. But this is a huge play, and it would be easy to get a little bit lost. To create an atmosphere where there is so much laughter and so much ease, and all the inhibitions have been broken down, is quite astonishing.'

Denis Quilley 'Because of John's collaborative approach the atmosphere in the rehearsal room is very relaxed, with lots of jokes and suggestions from the actors. It's only when a director is very confident and on top of it like John is that he can afford to allow this. Everyone's really enjoying themselves: although the work is very serious, it's not solemn, we don't have to be po-faced about it. I've enjoyed these rehearsals more than anything I've done for a long time.

'Nothing is being taken for granted, every line is being analysed for what it really means. This is difficult with a well-known play like *Hamlet*, because you think you know what the lines mean. But John has the gift of saying, Why can't it mean this, why can't we show it this way rather than that way? For my money it's paying off in spades: I think it's going to be a very fresh look at the play without being gimmicky, and without distorting its meaning and intention.'

Friday 23 June
During the week Simon and Sara have been making progress with the emotional heart of the play, the closet scene.

▼ ▼ ▼

Simon Russell Beale 'Yesterday I think we knocked it on the head. We did it three times, and I went for it full throttle, as Sara did. I was always terrified of it, so there was an enormous amount of beating around the bush before we got started. The third time we did it we were cooler, and I think that was the best version. The emotion was more natural, we didn't have to force it.

'With highly charged scenes like this one, the more emotionally wrapped up in it you are, the less good it is. I did desperately not want it to be maudlin or sexual. I don't necessarily buy in to the Oedipal thing, though it's a perfectly reasonable option. I don't think Hamlet wants to have sex with his mother, even subliminally; he just wants her to stop having sex with his uncle. I didn't want to be throwing her on the bed and that sort of stuff, because you don't treat your mother like that. Perhaps that's being terribly middle class, but to my mind the argument of the scene is more important than its physicality.

'It's such a complex relationship he has with his mother, and there are all sorts of reasons why he puts off going to her. One of the principal ones in my head is that he's frightened of the confrontation, he really doesn't want to have it. He finds it very difficult to say, You're a whore and a murderess, as anyone would. Especially as Sara is playing it from the beginning of the play as her having absolute concern for him. And then his instructions to his mother are so feeble. Confess yourself to heaven – Don't go to Claudius' bed – what good is that going to do? It would only alert Claudius and make him suspicious. So you get a feeling of, What good was it telling her, except for one's audit from heaven?

'At the end of the scene what is so devastating for me is that they're not separated. He's said what he has to say, and she still loves him. It's very sad, it would almost be better if they could wash their hands of each other and get on with their lives. But whereas Hamlet and Ophelia can determine their relationship, he and Gertrude can't, because a mother and son can't do that.'

John Caird 'There's nothing that worries me about Simon's progress as Hamlet, but inevitably he will become more dextrous with the text. He works from the big picture, which he gets in his head very clearly, and then develops the details. He's not one of those actors who starts with the details and then builds up slowly. That's what's wonderful with a part of such scale, he can have a clear idea of the map of the whole play because he's controlling it from the centre. But now I'm encouraging him to find more and more emotional and intellectual detail.'

Monday 26 June
Rehearsal room. Afternoon. Paul Pyant is present to check on lighting possibilities. The music, which is normally put in at the tech, is being inserted into the action for the first time, so John Cameron is on hand to see how his chosen Orlando Lasso motets fit in at different points.

The stage management team are increasingly in evidence. From her desk at one side of the rehearsal room, stage manager Trish Montemuro controls the pace of the rehearsal, continually reminding John to keep it moving so they can get through the day's schedule. The music is being controlled at another desk by the deputy stage manager, Fiona Bardsley. The assistant stage managers, Andrew and Valerie, are on constant call to move the trunks and suitcases – a task variously dubbed boxology or Trunkspotting.

▼ ▼ ▼

John Cameron 'Finding the Lasso motets has helped to give the play a setting that is completely different from other concepts of *Hamlet*. John's decision to lose all the political stuff makes it a much more cerebral production, it gives it a lightness and a floatiness, a more spiritual feeling which I'm trying to match in the original music I'm creating.

'In the old days directors could hold a tune in their head and talk to you about it, but they rarely had the kind of music skills that John has. His being a hands-on musician is a great advantage, he can feed off what he hears, he knows how music can be used in different ways.'

Paul Pyant 'With the lighting you have to think first and foremost about how best to tell the story. You try to service the production, and avoid any jiddery effects: there's nothing worse than coming out of a show humming the lighting or the set. So with each scene in *Hamlet* I need to know what time of day it is, where we are, what the weather's like, what kind of atmosphere we're trying to provide, and what that means for the set.

'John's good musical ear helps me in creating atmospheres. But he's not the sort of director who briefs you on the lighting. So it's been up to me to work out in rehearsal what his intentions are and what he wants the play to look like. Having worked with him on *Candide*, I've got to know his likes and dislikes. He tends to like quite painterly pictures, quite dramatic shifts.'

Wednesday 28 June
Rehearsal room. Morning. The actors are wearing different clothes, though not their own costumes. The men have put on jackets, the women have taken to long skirts, and Denis Quilley has found a cane for Polonius. Most of them are now off the book, and beginning to put more power as well as subtlety into their performances.

They work on joining Acts 2 and 3 together, then move on to the 'To be or not to be' scene. Simon speaks the soliloquy with great simplicity, sustaining its argument very clearly. John suggests that the first line is simply a repetition of what Hamlet has already concluded, and the idea emerges of Simon writing it down in his notebook before he starts the speech. John stresses that it begins casually – 'There's always the suicide option' – but then becomes more serious: 'It's not just about himself, it's not just about suicide, it's about existence.'

With Ophelia's arrival, there's a discussion about her attitude to this pre-arranged meeting. 'You need to play it knowing she's playing a scene she doesn't want to,' John suggests to Cathryn. Arising from this idea, it's decided that in response to Hamlet's question 'Where's your father?' she should let him know that Polonius is eavesdropping by shaking her head while replying 'At home, my lord'. This then makes more sense of Hamlet's subsequent fury.

▼ ▼ ▼

Simon Russell Beale 'Patsy Rodenburg has been helping me with the soliloquies. As a voice coach she's very good at seeing the whole arc of an argument. Quite often I get bogged down in the detail of a particular word, but she's very skilled at showing you how a thought may be five lines long rather than five separate thoughts, and pinning you down to that.

'But I haven't got the soliloquies right yet. "To be or not to be" is fine, it's a single arc. "Oh that this too too sullied flesh would melt" is a repressed, hysterical brood, but I think I'm in the right area, though technically it's a nightmare. But I'm not so sure what to do about "Oh what a rogue and peasant slave". It's very long, with three or four sections, and half way through I think I'm boring people to death. I don't know where Hamlet's brain is, so I'm trying it in different ways. Is this a man who can't feel anything, in which case you can play it as self-mocking throughout, or does he really feel something, then pulls back and says "Why what an ass am I"? It's a really tricky one.'

Patsy Rodenburg 'Simon has an incredible technique, but his brain moves so fantastically fast it's easy for him to get ahead of himself, and not connect emotionally. But he understands that, so we're working at reining him in and trying to break him of the habit. We're also looking at the meaning of the verse – not just the intellectual meaning, but the sensoral, visceral meaning. What is brilliant about Shakespeare is that form and content match, and that means that the shape of the word often releases something physically. We're exploring the physical structure of the verse, the iambic pentameter, the breaking of the thought and the line. Fortunately Simon absolutely understands the language, it's in his bloodstream, and that's a huge advantage.'

Friday 30 June
Rehearsal room. Afternoon. The company are working on the mad scene. Cathryn handles the violent shifts in Ophelia's thought-processes skilfully, her pure singing voice adding to the poignancy of the scene. John suggests that for her second entry she should wear her dead father's coat, drop it on the floor, and then re-enact his funeral using the coat as his body. 'It might be too literal, but let's try it,' he says.

The effect is moving and powerful, not least on Laertes, who is now witnessing not only his sister's madness, but a version of the burial that he missed. At the end of the scene John has the idea that Cathryn should push some of the low-hanging chandeliers, so that their swinging reflects her state of mind. It's a complicated manoeuvre to rehearse, with plastic buckets and makeshift pulleys standing in for the real thing.

Backtracking to Act 3, the actors work through its key scenes. Simon conveys a more steely Hamlet than before in the recorders speech to Rosencrantz and Guildernstern after the play; Peter works up a fine anguish in conveying Claudius' guilt in his 'O my offence is rank' soliloquy; and Sara and Simon take another emotional roller-coaster ride through the closet scene.

Afterwards John gives some general notes. 'That's a very fine chunk, we've made good progress. What we need to do now is run it, so we have a section that more or less works. The big job is going to be rhythmic, and we can't tell how that's working until we run scene for scene. So next week is going to be an education for us.'

▼ ▼ ▼

Cathryn Bradshaw 'I was frightened of the mad scene, because if you don't hit it properly it can be very embarrassing. But I got a lot from seeing a mad woman on a train the other day. I've been using gestures she used – for instance she did a lot of stamping. She was so vehement, and I've been trying to catch the intensity of her contact with people. It really helped me, seeing someone who was on her own track, yet saying quite profound things. You couldn't make any sense of it, but she obviously had a theme.

'One of the problems with Ophelia is to decide whether she has a theme, whether in the mad scene she's gone in there to tell people specific things, or whether they're just coming out of her inner life. I think it's the latter, even though they say she's importunate, that she needs to see the queen. I don't think she has any rationale for it. I want to give the impression of someone who is "home alone" – no parental control any more, no brother, no one to turn to. I imagine her up in the middle of the night, not eating, and losing track of life.'

Sara Kestelman 'When we did the mad scene this morning it was the first time for a week. Cathy is astonishing in it, and we got very, very upset. I couldn't stop crying, but John rightly said, You have to stop, you have to find a way of feeling it when it's appropriate and not falling apart, of finding the steel in the character. Ophelia is in her own bubble, you're not in it with her, and you have to fight not to be. It was a brilliant note to give, because it means you have to investigate those areas of your character that will steel you against crying.

'Like a lot of observing roles Gertrude is a slow burn for the actor. Last week I thought, I hope everyone doesn't think I'm trailing here, because I am, I'm way behind. But I can only catch up by listening and watching and absorbing, and hoping that some stuff begins to happen.'

Monday 3 July
In addition to working on the detail of their speeches with some of the actors, Stephen has been working with the understudies.

▼ ▼ ▼

Stephen Wrentmore 'I try to make sure that no one in the production is ignored, so for example with Chris Staines and Paul Bazely I've been sorting out the relationship between Rosencrantz and Guildernstern, because they're such a tricky pair. I've been working with Guy on Laertes' emotional journey, which is a hellish job for him because most of it happens offstage. And I've worked a little with Cathy on the mad scene, though John has been very focussed on that, so I'm just picking up the end of it.

'The main difficulty with working with the understudies is time. In this production essentially there are 16 people on stage all the time, and I need to be working with eight of them in another room. You just have to fit them in somehow: part of the philosophy of the National is that understudies are thoroughly rehearsed, it's not just a matter of, "Learn the part and on you go."

'In the case of Simon Day, who's understudying Hamlet, it's especially important to fit him in with the choreography of the production, while helping him to invest independently in the part, and we've been exploring that together.'

Simon Day 'I'm meant to be off the book by the first preview, and I think I'll just about be there. I've been working quite a lot with Stephen on certain speeches, but once the previews are out of the way we'll be able to have proper sessions and run whole scenes.

'It's difficult rehearsing Hamlet while I'm also rehearsing Horatio, as they're on stage together so much. A lot of the time the motto is, Keep your lips together. I've gone back to something I used to do in drama school, which is highlighting the text – blue for Horatio, pink for Hamlet. Unless I can see the two parts in separate colours, there are bound to be scenes I'll mess up.

'I have to play the part in a way that won't throw any of the other actors. But to attempt a slavish imitation of Simon's Hamlet would be wrong, and also impossible. Of course I haven't been thinking, Should I play it on crutches or as a Martian? I'm just trying to fit my personality into the situation, and see what I would do under those circumstances.

'I think the soliloquies are the key, because they're Hamlet stripped bare, talking through his thoughts and feelings. They provide stepping stones, and if you can get them right, then everything else falls into place.'

Wednesday 5 July
Rehearsal rooom. Afternoon. The company are re-visiting Act 1. With just a fortnight until the technical Trish pushes the rehearsal on at a swifter pace. 'Play it for the full emotional value,' John tells the actors, who proceed to do so. The work is more intense, there are fewer gags now. Simon is much more contained, more submerged in Hamlet's world: his fear seems palpable as he listens to the Ghost tell his story.

Laertes' farewell has been set on a quayside, demanding an immensely complex scene change. But the trunkshifting, planned in minute detail by the stage management, is beginning to work more smoothly, and the energy the actors use to move the set gives extra pace to the story.

John Cameron is in attendance again, to see where the music might need cutting or extending. Three musicians are also present, with recorders to provide live music for the play scene. As the company works through the cues it becomes clear that more music is required in at least two places, in one instance because lines originally cut have been restored.

▼ ▼ ▼

John Cameron 'The challenge with the original music has been to find a style that reflects the Lasso, but which also has a contemporary feeling. I've always been a great fan of late medieval and renaissance music, but I didn't want to go just into the renaissance, I wanted to use its sonorities in a twentieth-century way.

'It's not like writing a movie score, you don't want to overstate it. In the theatre you have to be more detached and subtle, to try to gauge the music so it sits very lightly with the production, and enhances it without ever being obtrusive.'

John Caird 'In a part the size of Hamlet you can rehearse each scene until the cows come home, but it only starts to make total sense and reveal itself fully after you've run it several times. Then you can start making adjustments in how you pace it, and see what it's telling you at different moments in the story. For as well as performing *it*, it starts to perform *you*. The character starts telling the actor what it wants, and begins to have a life. Provided an actor is receptive and responsive to those demands, the relationship between character and actor becomes increasingly productive.

'Simon is becoming more and more impressive. The way he holds the whole play together in his imagination is quite extraordinary. His fascination for the development of the character, his appetite for experiment, and his daring as an actor are constantly astonishing. He lives on the experience of driving the play through with his will and passion and fire. He's like a racehorse at the start of the Grand National: every time we go into a single scene or a run of part of the play, he can't wait to get at it.'

Denis Quilley 'Simon is not most people's idea of how Hamlet should look. But although he's not tall and willowy and conventionally pretty, he's very attractive. His intelligence and wit and emotional directness are among the things that make him attractive, as well as his nice face.

'The great thing is that he always comes to a part with a clean slate, with no preconceptions based on what other actors have done with a part - his Iago was a good example of that. Here he's said, Let's forget Gielgud and Olivier and John Neville, and just see what the character means. I think he's going to be an exceptional Hamlet – and I don't often say that kind of thing at this stage in rehearsals.'

Tuesday 11 July
Rehearsal room. Afternoon. The first complete run-through. John explains that
the lights won't be sorted out until the technical, but that today the music will be
integrated as fully as possible. He warns the actors that it will be louder than in
the theatre, but also that it's still negotiable, that their opinions will affect
decisions still to be made.

Meanwhile he's looking for pace and concentration: 'Keep it buzzy, but not
racing, keep it performance size,' he says. 'Don't get lost in your own problems:
you must be in the moment for yourself in your character, but the minute you
stop the scene, watch the rest of the play, get a sense of its atmosphere, so
that you know what its true nature is when you next walk on the stage as
your character.'

The run-through is impressive, both technically and emotionally. There are few
dries or missed cues, the scenes are knitting well together, and the music lifts the
performance to another plane. Suddenly there is a true ensemble feeling, and the
thematic logic of the play seems beautifully clear. Simon is now in control of his
soliloquies: the difficulties of 'Oh what a rogue and peasant slave' have vanished,
and he gives it a subtle, assured rendering.

John is delighted. 'That was very impressive, a real quantum leap,' he says.
'Where we got to today is where we have to get to in performance. The move to
the theatre will tend to knock us off our perch, but this is what we have to hang
on to, this is sacrosanct.'

He offers the actors advice about the technical rehearsal. 'The tech will tune the
house to your voices and your spirits. But part of your job is to sit and watch your
peers at work, to get a sense of how they look on stage. So go up to the circle, or
come and sit with us in the stalls: don't let the proscenium arch and the pass door
get in the way.'

Trish asks the actors to make a list of any problems they have, and reminds them
of the schedule for the rest of the week: three days of technicals, tomorrow,
Thursday and Friday, dress rehearsals Friday night and Saturday afternoon, and
the first preview Saturday evening. It sounds an exhausting schedule, and John is
sceptical: 'I don't ever remember having one dress rehearsal at the National, never
mind two.'

▼ ▼ ▼

John Caird 'The first complete run-through is always a very important moment. It's the time when the actors start to feel how their journey through the play fits together and makes sense for them, and so will ultimately make sense and be satisfying for an audience.

'You find that things that seemed all right when you were rehearsing scenes on their own now feel less appropriate. A run-through also gives you a chance to add elements of story-telling and character that you'd perhaps missed, and make thematic connections between the actions of characters and ideas shared between different plots.'

Simon Russell Beale 'I was pleased with the run-through. In the gap when Hamlet goes to England, I'd been going off and having a fag and a glass of water, and losing my concentration. I suddenly became aware of that, and today I got it back.

'I also began to get the feel of him being a changed man when he returns. Before, he's reacting to things a lot, he has very firm stimuli like the Ghost and the Players to react to. But after England he shuts off, he stops soliloquising, and you've got to find a reason for him doing that. Does he not want to communicate with his friends the audience, or does he feel no need to communicate with them? I believe it's the latter. And at what point does he resign himself to death? I think that comes early in the fifth act, soon after his return. If he discovers it too late, the fight becomes less irrelevant.

'The tech days can be an incredibly useful period. The most important thing is that you keep working on your performance, and don't just sit back and work on technical things. I'm still honing ideas that I've had, some of which are very fresh and new, so they've not yet been thought through properly.'

Patsy Rodenburg 'To help the company with the move into the theatre from the rehearsal room I've been working with them on their voices, getting strength in them, extending their capacity and range, so they have a big landscape to play on vocally, and can handle the text as it becomes more heightened.

'The trouble with most British theatre is that we rehearse in a room with a wall where the energy is very limited, and the actors then go into a big space and think they've lost their performance. And of course the rehearsal room is acoustically alive, so when they go into a dead theatre they panic, and start pushing or over-emoting. My priority is to do warm-ups for the first few shows, so they begin to understand the different energy the theatre requires. That's why the previews are so important.'

Thursday 13 July
The Lyttelton theatre auditorium. Evening. The last session of the second day of the technical rehearsal. Trish and John are directing operations. John is sitting at a desk placed in the middle of the stalls, with lighting designer Paul Pyant and sound designer Christopher Shutt at computerised monitors beside him. Tim Hatley and John Cameron are also on hand nearby.

Trish moves constantly between the stalls and the stage as problems arise, in touch via her headphones with her team backstage, as well as with Fiona in the control box at the back of the stalls. On stage the actors seem suddenly distant, and briefly unrecognisable in their full-blown costumes. While they work through the scenes, a running conversation about the sound, lighting and music takes place in the stalls between John and his team.

'The chandeliers are beautiful, but do they dominate the action?'
'Could we make the jig about 50% faster?'
'Let's have a green up on the white.'
'I think we should move the trunk about six inches upstage.'
'Backlight the cross, it looks too neony.'
'Don't start the iron [safety curtain] until the music reaches the tonic.'
'The colour is still work-in-progress, it looks too equatorial.'

The play scene is worked on in great detail. Ophelia needs more light downstage left. The height of certain chandeliers needs adjusting. The recorder music needs to be speeded up. But the changes are not purely technical. John is worried that the visual device used to suggest Claudius' guilt is not working: 'We're losing the mirror image with the hands,' he says. 'Let's do something really tricky, and have Gertrude rising and the Player Queen moving forward at the same time.'

Despite the long day, the actors patiently accept the constant interruptions and endless adjustments. Trish maintains a balance between problem-solving and keeping the rehearsal moving.

▼ ▼ ▼

Trish Montemuro 'For the technical I knew we would have to do a lot with the flying of the chandeliers, and it has been quite difficult. We have about 19 flying cues, and we've needed a lot of time to decide what configuration they should be in for each scene, which involved discussion with Tim, John and Paul. So beforehand we made sure we'd done all the box changes in detail, and had a list made of each actor's movements with them.

'Simon's performance has grown enormously: you see little grains happening, and then they build into something very powerful, such as the end of the closet scene. Usually I get bored with Hamlet's angst, but he makes it such a human journey, everyone can relate to it. It also lacks vanity, which you often see with Hamlet. I think it's going to be a very special performance.'

3.   *The Previews*

T he actors now face the first of six previews. It is, John stresses, a critical moment. 'The longer you rehearse a play, the more involved the actors become in the detail of their own performances and of their relationship on stage with the other actors. Those relationships become more and more exclusive of outside enjoyment, so the first previews are something of a shock to them, because they've gone deeper and deeper, and so further and further away from their own first reactions to the play.'

Before the performance he offers the actors a word of caution: 'I know you're never going to give any less than 100%, but for the moment try to keep 5-10% of your minds out of your performance, so you can spend time observing what you're doing. Part of your responsibility during this preview period is to talk to me and each other about how it's going, and you can't do that if you're getting completely bound up in your performance.'

The evening's performance before a full house in the Lyttelton goes extremely well. There are no serious technical problems, the scene-changes go like clockwork, and the actors respond to the rapt stillness of the audience with an assured and confident performance. Simon's Hamlet is clear, witty, swift and poignant; in the soliloquies he has the audience in the palm of his hand; at the end there is sustained applause and loud cheers. Afterwards in the green room the main feeling is one of relief, that this first difficult hurdle has been successfully cleared. But Simon, though pleased, is cautious: 'You have to be careful, preview audiences are always on your side, and the first one is not typical.'

Thursday 20 July
The morning after the fourth preview. The actors are gathered in the front row of the Lyttelton stalls for John's notes. Last night's running time was 3 hours 15 minutes, five minutes longer than Monday's. John is not happy, and delivers a stern lecture.

'Those extra five minutes are serious, and need our attention. Last night you were falling into patterns of speech, putting inflections on lines or phrases without thinking about it. It's the kind of thing that doesn't normally happen until you're in a long run. There was also a lot of emotional generalisation – In this speech I'll be sad, and so on. When this happens you start singing, your vowels get longer, and you buy yourself a little more time. It's as if you'd rather be in an opera.

'There were quite a few fluffs, and spoonerisms, and lines being thrown. The reason was that you were not connecting with each other. You were listening to yourself, and not enough to others. You were digging away in your own character, so you were less infected by the language. You were doing things to the words, rather than letting them do things to you.

'I know there is tiredness, which is understandable. But I'm going to be brutal, I'm not going to let you do this patterning, because it's catching, and it can become competitive. The solution lies in the power of thought. Take care of the thoughts, and the emotions will look after themselves. If you're truly thinking, you'll never find the same pattern, except by chance. So police it, be merciless with yourselves. It's essential that your thoughts stay fresh, that you keep them sizzling away beneath you. Get your pulses racing from the half, don't go on with cotton wool in your mouth.

'We must avoid long-run-itis, we have to be intellectually excited every night. This is a remarkable and wonderful play that we're going to be carting round the world. You've got to wake up in the morning and think, It's *Hamlet* today! Otherwise what are we here for?'

He then gives individual notes, adjusting a move here, pinpointing a loss of concentration there. The actors spend the rest of the morning refining these details on stage. Afterwards there's praise for John's forthright talk. 'It was really helpful,' Cathryn says. 'You try to police yourself and be a third eye, but if you do it too much you're outside of what you're doing, and then it all goes wrong anyway. So you need someone like John to be that honest. Not everyone would bother to tell you.'

Friday 21 July
The lecture has had an effect: last night two minutes were taken off the previous night's running time. John is clearly pleased that the actors have responded to his criticisms.

'The performance last night was extraordinarily alive and fresh, and underivative of anything they'd ever done before. Of course new patterns may emerge, and they too will have to be got rid of. The great difficulty actors have with the first few previews is their own comfort. After the arduous business of rehearsal and the technicals they're emotionally exhausted, and the repetitiveness of the work is enervating. In that state their choices can sometimes become motivated by safety and comfort, rather than by the daring and risk they should be involved in.

'It actually happens when an entire cast feels comfortable with the work. In a troubled company that's at odds with itself, where some people have fared much better than others, it won't be so apparent, because people are still trying to experiment themselves out of their own unhappiness. But in a company like this one, where everyone is more or less at the same level of performance and understanding of the play, the patterns can be set up much earlier. In fact it's quite a good thing that they have been, because now they can get them out of their system.'

The previews have given the technical team a chance to consider whether any scenes or moments need re-thinking. Seeing the lighting or hearing the music in continuous action for only the second or third time, they're able to tighten up or change aspects of the production at several points.

Saturday 22 July
The final preview. After today there's to be a week's break, then the start of the tour at Malvern, followed by the trip to Elsinore. As the press night is not until early September, when the company returns to the Lyttelton, John suggests they treat tonight's performance as the opening, and use it for all the normal first-night rituals, exchanging good-luck cards and so on. In this way he hopes they will feel the show has already opened when they get to Malvern, and that the London press night will then be more of an ordinary night, when the press just happen to be there.

The audience reaction to the evening's performance is as enthusiastic as it has been throughout the week. Afterwards Simon reflects on the value of the previews. 'Their main use is to just get you through the play. The first one was pretty good, I thought we were rather well prepared, but there's been a lot of fine tuning since then. For instance, tonight we changed the blocking for the closet scene. It had seemed all right in the rehearsal room, but on stage it seemed too static. There's more movement now, and that's released us emotionally. I've also begun to get more of a sense of the shape of the play, the rising graph that goes up to the point when Hamlet goes to England, and then this extraordinary last act, which is almost like a separate play.

'Someone told me I was a very cerebral Hamlet. I think what he meant was that there wasn't a lot of hysteria in my performance. Hysteria has its place, and wonderful Hamlets have been much more emotionally expressive than me. But every Hamlet is different. My response to him is not what I expected it to be. I thought it would be more savage, more grotesque and less self-assured. But I seem to have found a great calm in him.'

John is also very satisfied with the week's work. 'Previews are always deeply instructive. There's a well-known theatre axiom that the audience is the missing character in any play you're doing. In a Shakespeare play that's probably more true than in others, because the story is so full of soliloquy. So many characters have a relationship with the missing character, that when you get an audience for the first time you complete the circle of communication, and find what the play needs in order to have a meaning. Consciously or otherwise, actors learn a tremendous amount from a live audience, about attention, about timing, about tension.'

He feels Simon has benefitted a great deal from these first six performances. 'In a positive and creative way he's fallen in love with the audience. I think it's a necessary part of his journey. To arrive in front of an audience and have them so manifestly and audibly appreciative must have been music to his ears. He's bound to be seduced by their response, but as he's an honest player he won't be corrupted by it. Over the next few weeks he'll continue to play with the audience, but he'll become more rigorous in the way he does so. The great risk in the first few previews in a big, romantic part is self-indulgence. But Simon is an extremely self-denying actor, so I don't think he'll ever be guilty of that.'

'My response to Hamlet is not what I expected:
I seem to have found a great calm in him.'

Simon Russell Beale

Rehearsal and production photographs by Catherine Ashmore

Above: Sara Kestelman: 'Like a lot of observing roles, Gertrude is a slow burn for the actor.'

Right: Peter McEnery: 'I'm more interested in the denial in Claudius' character, the fact that he doesn't want to face his crime.'

Left: Cathryn Bradshaw: 'Ophelia is often seen as passive throughout, but I want to get away from that.'

Top: Denis Quilley (with Ken Oxtoby, Barnardo/Priest): 'Polonius is conceited and a bit of a bore, but he's not an idiot; in fact he's a consummate manipulator.'

Above: John Caird, with Simon Russell Beale: 'Simon's fascination for the development of the character, his appetite for experiment, and his daring as an actor are constantly astonishing.'

Left: Sylvester Morand (Player King) and Janet Spencer-Turner
(Player Queen)

Top: Simon Day (Horatio)

Above: Guy Lankester (Laertes)

Top left: Edward Gower (Reynaldo/Francisco)

Top right: Martin Chamberlain (Marcellus), Christopher Staines (Rosencrantz), Paul Bazely (Guildenstern)

Above: Michael Wildman (Osric/Player), Chloe Angharad (Gentlewoman/Player)

Right: John Caird: 'You have to give actors the What and the Why, but never the How.' *(inset)* Stephen Wrentmore (Staff Director)

Left: 'Angels and ministers of grace defend us!'

Above: 'O, my offence is rank, it smells to heaven.'

Right: 'Come, my coach. Good night, ladies, good night.'

Top: 'He poisons him i' th'garden for his estate. His name
is Gonzago.'

Above: 'Be thou familiar, but by no means vulgar.'

Left: 'Laertes, was your father dear to you?'

Top: 'I must be cruel only to be kind'

Above: 'A hit, a very palpable hit.'

Above: 'The Scripture says Adam digged. Could he dig
without arms?'

Right: 'I knew him, Horatio, a fellow of infinite jest, of most
excellent fancy.'

4. *The Tour Begins*

Wednesday 2 August   Malvern, Worcestershire. The actors have arrived in this small, attractive spa town, strung out along the hills overlooking the Severn Valley. Tonight the *Hamlet* tour begins with the first of ten performances in the Festival theatre.

Jenny Mann, the National's tour publicist, is mounting the production photographs in the theatre foyer. Her role in publicising these first performances, and those soon to come in Brighton and Glasgow, is complicated by the fact that the press night is not until next month. 'Without review quotes, I'm lacking part of the weaponry I usually have to sell a show,' she says. 'There's a brief comment today in a preview paragraph in the *Guardian*, describing Simon as 101% brilliant. But that's a bit unofficial, so I can't use it in an ad, though I could perhaps in a mailing letter. But protocol is a delicate thing. We've asked the press to come to the Lyttelton in September, but these performances in Malvern are not previews, nothing about them is embargoed, so there's nothing to stop a critic coming along. Fortunately they usually respect what we ask of them.'

During the morning Stephen holds a word-run in the modern Forum theatre, across the foyer from the Festival theatre. The actors have had a ten-day break from the play, and need to re-acquaint themselves with the text, and each other. With no lights, music or sound, and chairs standing in for boxes on the bare stage, there's no attempt to give a proper performance: the aim is simply to get the lines right, pick up cues promptly, and get back under the skin of the characters. The run also serves as an informal re-bonding session, and the playing is light and casual. More than a hint of camp is allowed to creep in, and in the the last scene, played up to the melodramatic hilt, the gags begin to come. Hamlet's dying words 'let it be' provoke a collective hum of the Lennon/McCartney song. The mood at the end is merry and relaxed, as was intended.

In the afternoon it's back to reality, and the technical rehearsal. The small, late-Victorian theatre poses an immense challenge after the larger space in the Lyttelton. Since Sunday the production and stage management teams have been in the theatre, where lighting has been one of the major problems. 'It's been a pretty tense few days, and a lot of midnight oil has been burnt getting the new plan right,' Paul Pyant says. 'The stage is a quarter of the size, and we've brought less than a third of the set. Only some of the back wall has come, and the side walls have been cut completely. We haven't got room for all the boxes, and we've only got 18 chandeliers out of 30. So it's all very scaled down. But we've tried to keep the principal lighting elements of each scene.'

The tech throws up problems for the actors. With no side walls, fewer entrances, and no space to cross behind the cyclorama, the feeling is slightly claustrophobic. The stage gets very crowded in some of the scene changes, which need careful re-rehearsing. ('It's ages since I did pub theatre,' one actor remarks.) Because of the rake everyone has to be careful with their movement, especially Simon and Guy in the fight scene. Sometimes they mask each other in the smaller space, so Stephen darts around the stage, suggesting new positions. Occasionally they are unable to hear their cues because the music is too loud. A huge amount of adjustment is needed.

In the evening the Malvern audience becomes totally absorbed in the performance. At the end they stand, applauding and cheering loudly. Afterwards the actors receive many enthusiastic comments as they mingle with members of the audience at a buffet reception in the theatre's restaurant.

Friday 4 August
The first reviews appear, in the local and regional press. They are extremely positive. John's production is applauded for its care and inspiration, while Simon's Hamlet attracts widespread praise for its intelligence and clarity. But one paper headlines its review 'Tubby or not tubby, fat is the question', a witticism which Simon finds a little hurtful. 'It wouldn't be so bad if it was just slipped in during the article,' he says ruefully.

John is not happy with the decision to bring the production to such a small theatre. 'While everything is smaller or closer together, the actors are still the same size, so the effect is a Brobdignagian version of *Hamlet*. It looks muddled, like a rehearsal-room fit-up production with an unnecessarily elaborate backwall device. Or it looks like a nice design that hasn't been quite completed, as if we couldn't afford the sides. I feel the show should either be done with its three walls and 15 openings and clear delineation of a prison-like interior space that could be a church, all the evocative things that the set in the Lyttelton expresses – or we shouldn't have the walls at all, we should just use the metaphor of the trunks and lamps, and get on with it. Luckily in Trish we've got the most organised and persuasive stage manager in the history of stage management, so things have gone very smoothly here.'

Saturday 12 August
The last night at Malvern. Overall, despite the problems with the set, the ten days here have been a success. Simon is delighted with the audience reaction. 'It was good, very friendly, and much more vocal than I had imagined.' But his feelings are less positive about the move from the Lyttelton to the smaller theatre: 'I didn't particularly like the mix and match feeling of it. The stage was a bit crowded, and the production lost something with half the chandeliers gone. On the other hand the smaller space made the play more intimate, which was useful: you could take your foot off the pedal.'

After the performance ends, Trish and her team supervise the striking of the set, and along with Stephen prepare to fly out tomorrow to Denmark.

Sunday 13 August
Kronborg Castle, Elsinore. Here, exactly four hundred years after its first performance, the actors are to perform *Hamlet* in the very castle in which Shakespeare set the play. The building is quite unlike the Gothic, gloomy place high above the sea that everyone had been expecting. Built in the Dutch Renaissance style in warm, Cotswold-coloured stone, with a lighthouse beacon shining at night from one of its towers, the castle stands at sea level on the edge of the Sound, the strip of water that separates Denmark from Sweden. There is in fact no direct evidence that Shakespeare ever visited Elsinore, although members of his company, the Chamberlain's Men, certainly did so. Scholars and critics remain divided over whether the many local references in the text are based on direct observation by Shakespeare, or on reports from his fellow-actors.

There has not been a production of *Hamlet* here for ten years. Recent ones, including those starring Kenneth Branagh and David Threlfall, have been staged on the battlements rather than in the courtyard where the National company will be performing. The stage being set up in one corner of the yard is nearer in size and shape to the Olivier than the Lyttelton, with its 680 seats spread round three sides on a steeply banked, purpose-built scaffolding construction.

The control box is behind the back row, under a tarpaulin cover, alongside two spotlights: otherwise the stage is lit by a series of tall rigs placed around the courtyard. The set is minimal: there is no back wall, and so no cross, and no crack for characters to step through from the real world. The task of adapting the production for these very different conditions is complicated by the absence of both director and designer. It had always been intended that Stephen should supervise this part of the tour on John's behalf. But it had also been assumed that Tim, who had already come out on a reconnoitring trip, would be on hand to supervise the re-design. His enforced absence has put considerable extra pressure on Stephen, who now has to make crucial design as well as directing decisions. One of these has involved a disagreement with the festival organiser, who didn't like the flats that had been put up, and wanted the production to be played against the castle walls. 'That's a different production of *Hamlet*,' Stephen explains. 'This isn't a play about Denmark; this is a play about a man. Elsinore is just a device.'

Tuesday 15 August
The actors and musicians arrive in Elsinore in the late afternoon, and are driven almost immediately from their accommodation to the castle, to start the technical rehearsal in the new venue in preparation for tomorrow night's opening. Also in the party are Jenny Mann, Roger Chapman, the National's Head of Touring, and Head of Press Lucinda Morrison, who's here to look after two British journalists writing features on the production.

The tech begins in daylight, and continues as darkness falls. One immediate problem is communication within the stage management team, whose headphones only work poorly in the open air because of interference. Another is the actors' visibility to the audience as they leave the stage and walk the few yards to the dressing-room in the castle. Originally their movements were covered by screens, but the local fire officer has insisted on a five-metre gap between the castle and the stage, and they have had to come down. As a compromise, two side flats have been erected to mask the movements of the actors standing backstage.

With no time to recuperate after travelling for most of the day, the actors are cold, exhausted and obviously stressed. Then, as they rehearse the closet scene, Sylvester enters in the guise of the Ghost, gliding on to the stage in unexpectedly smooth style on a micro-scooter hidden beneath his cloak. The actors collapse with laughter, and the tension is broken.

Afterwards Simon ponders the challenges that face him and the company in this historic venue. 'My main worry is the sheer size of the stage, which means you lose many of the subtleties. Although it was calm this evening, I'm told the wind can take your voice right away. I've never played outside before, and I'm worried about the physical effort, the need to be much more rhetorical. Even tonight I got bored with the sound of my own voice, because you have to do it at such a pitch. But it's a thrilling place to be playing in. I found it very exciting as the light was dying, and you got all the different colours of the sky. At one point I went to the loo and came back through the dark and I thought, I'm Hamlet, and I'm walking through Elsinore!'

Wednesday 16 August

A brief press call at Lo-Skolen, the conference centre where the company is staying. The mayor, Per Taersbol, dressed casually in jeans, turns out to be a former actor who once played Hamlet. He explains that after a break of several years in the tradition of companies doing *Hamlet* at Elsinore, the town now plans to stage a production every year.

The actors field questions from local journalists: Simon emphasises the domestic nature of the National's production, while Denis suggests that cutting out the politics has improved the play. After lunch they return to the castle, where the crew are uncovering the stage after this morning's rain and, in the face of a strong wind, Jenny is setting up the publicity boards at the entrance to the courtyard.

Trish and Roger Chapman have had a difficult meeting with the festival producer Terence Davies. Without insurance, which was too costly, he's nervous about any interruption that might lead to postponement or cancellation, and wants to be able to sit backstage in order to be party to any such decision. Trish and Roger, however, feel the actors' safety is paramount, and that she should be the one to halt or postpone the action if need be. 'You can't have a committee meeting about stopping a show,' she explains. Their view has prevailed.

One necessity during the tech is to get the new box moves right. But the greatest problem is audibility. The castle is still open to visitors, so that as well as seagulls and the occasional plane, the actors have to contend with the noise of groups of Japanese tourists and Danish schoolchildren, who walk through the courtyard and behind the stage area on their tour of the building. Stephen, running up to the back row from time to time, warns the actors if and when their words are lost.

Unlike in the Lyttelton or at Malvern, the actors have to negotiate steps on to the raised stage. This means careful re-rehearsing of certain entries, such as the carrying of Ophelia's bier into the graveyard. There are a couple of minor injuries: Denis cuts his hand while he's inside the grave, and Janet Spencer-Turner, the Player Queen, is stung on the foot by a bee, causing her to walk with a visible limp.

Just as Simon comes to 'The readiness is all' it begins to rain, the tech is abandoned, and the stage hastily covered again. The actors huddle in the dressing rooms, a series of bare, dank vaulted rooms within the castle directly behind the stage. Though spacious enough, they have no running water, which means a kettle has to be boiled in order to be able to get the Ghost's make-up off.

Here Trish offers the actors some last-minute advice. She warns them they may have problems in seeing their floor markings in the darker scenes, and to be careful with their footing once the dew descends towards the end of the evening. She also explains the scenario if, as now seems likely, rain should interrupt the performance: 'I might let a bit of drizzle go, but I won't let it get dangerous,' she says.

Miraculously, the heavy rain stops an hour before the scheduled start, and the show begins on time under a clear, pale-blue sky. The audience, laced with local dignitaries, is at first slow to react, and there's noticeably no response to the line 'Denmark is a prison'. As the play proceeds the open air gives a special resonance to references to the elements, though not always at the right moment: Hamlet's allusion to the 'brave o'erhanging firmament' is made in broad daylight. As Simon reaches 'Oh what a rogue and peasant slave' the handful of clouds in the sky are turning to pink, and by the time he arrives at 'To be or not to be' it is dusk. A rare jet plane drowns Hamlet and Ophelia's 'country matters' exchange, but otherwise only the occasional shrieking of a gull and the chiming of the clock tower disturb the action.

During the interval members of the audience wrap themselves up in blankets lent by the local fire brigade. Night thickens, and thus protected from the biting cold they become increasingly enthralled by the action unfolding under the starlit Danish sky. Their response at the end is full of warmth and enthusiam.

Afterwards the actors attend a candlelit buffet reception in the castle's magnificent banqueting hall. Later, walking through the castle grounds alongside the moat lit every few yards with flares, with a full moon shining above the silhouetted walls and towers, they talk about the magic of acting in the famous courtyard. Paul Bazely says: 'It's wonderful not to have to think a scene in your head, but to be actually playing it here.' Cathryn adds: 'It took me a while to settle down, but when I was waiting to go on for the mad scene it came upon me how thrilling it was.'

Simon is equally enthusiastic: 'It was a fantastic occasion, and wonderful to see the sky and relate it to the play. Because you were in the open air you felt you were talking about the whole world, about God, about everything. There were noises, but unless it was very loud, like the planes, I was unaware of it. The bells didn't worry me, or the birds or the wind or the sea; they were all part of the soundscape.' But he was less certain about his performance. 'I honestly didn't know whether it was good or bad, I just aimed to get through it. Until the interval I was scared of the audience; I prefer them to be well out of sight. Also I was oddly outside myself, I was feeling slightly remote, and thinking it was a bit of a weird thing to be doing, standing and shouting on a stage.'

Stephen is generally satisfied with the Elsinore opening. 'The actors were a bit scared at the start, it's an enormous stage which involves a lot of walking. With a new venue there's always a sense of tiptoeing back into the play. I think tonight Simon was slightly on the back foot for the first few speeches. But overall it went very well. The elements that didn't quite work were because we were outside. The opening, for instance, where the actors are seen to be ghosts, only really makes sense in the dark; here it just looked like a line-up of the cast. The other thing we've lost because of the open auditorium is John and Tim's concept of the enclosure, that end-on view where you look into the box, and the only knowledge of the outside world is the small chink at the back, where there's life rather than death. Only when it became dark did we begin to get that back.'

Thursday 17 August
Over breakfast, in the cold light of day, the actors reflect on last night's performance. Most of them disliked playing the first part in daylight: 'It produces rather unsubtle acting,' Janet says. 'I don't like seeing people's wig lines and their make-up. When I first came on there was a clash of colours in the audience which put the actors out of focus. It was also rather distracting seeing a woman breastfeeding her baby.' Simon Day enjoyed speaking his line 'Flights of angels sing thee to thy rest' to the elements, but found the conditions difficult. 'The

stage was very damp with dew, and you felt a bit hammy hitting every consonant really hard, like an RSC actor.' Sara found it physically very demanding and hard to project: 'If someone told me I'd never have to play in Elsinore again, I'd be secretly very pleased,' she admits.

There's also some concern about the actors' visibility between the flats, which seems especially awkward when the 'dead' Polonius is seen returning to the dressing-room. Denis suggests it might have been better to have had no flats, and have the actors sitting on chairs at the side of the stage, 'so at least you were making a statement'.

At noon, in bright sunshine, the company arrives at the Marienlyst Hotel near the castle for a reception given by members of the National's development department. On the terrace looking across to Sweden they mingle with a group of the theatre's financial supporters who have been brought over from London for twenty-four hours to see the production, then join them for an excellent lunch inside.

6.30 in the evening. The castle courtyard. During the afternoon there's been a thunderstorm and torrential rain, but now it's finally stopped, and right on cue the sky is clearing. The crew are sweeping the water from the stage, while others are drying the seats with towels and sponges. The actors stand around anxiously, getting individual notes from Stephen, who is again stressing the importance of being heard.

Once again, the show goes on. This time the performance is more assured and relaxed, the audience more responsive, and the rapport between them and the actors more evident. Simon plays with confidence, giving Hamlet more bite without losing his other qualities; after 'O what a rogue and peasant slave' he gets a round of applause. The heavens more obviously become another character in the play, making its spiritual qualities sharper. The reception at the end borders on the tumultuous. 'They cracked it,' Stephen says as the audience vanishes into the night. 'They established a relationship with the audience from the beginning. I feel they're back on top of it.'

At supper afterwards the actors are clearly pleased: they know they've regained control of the play. Simon senses a significant improvement. 'In general I'm unaware of whether a performance is more or less powerful, but tonight I felt it was much better played by everybody,' he says. 'The pace was different, the audience was less formal, they got the jokes from the beginning. So we were more relaxed, and we did a proper show.'

Friday 18 August
Over breakfast Simon talks about Hamlet's faith, and how far his own tentative religious feelings have informed his performance. 'I suppose my faith is borderline really, it's been building up for years, and it's time I jumped one way or the other. But I think it affects my playing of the part enormously, and of course my personal circumstances, the death of my mother, make it especially important.

'The play is unquestionably Hamlet's debate with his God, and where that leads him in the final act is probably to a good place. That's what it's been most nights; there's that whole sense that all will be well. Perhaps that's too sentimental, but I think it's a valid reading. I think his line "I am dead, Horatio" is a happy line, because he's meeting his God. I'm playing around with giving it a smile, but it might change every night, depending where I've got to in his journey. I might sometimes feel more resigned, abdicating responsibility and judgement for my own life, or it might be a wonderful moment of happiness and release – or both.'

Thursday 24 August
The last of the eight performances at Elsinore. This time the torrential rain comes later, and prevents a prompt start. Some of the actors don't want to go ahead, but others are keen not to cancel. Eventually the skies clear, and despite it being bitterly cold, with a high wind causing the lighting towers to sway and the tarpaulins to flap noisily, the decision is made to risk going ahead. Darkness is falling, and a deal is struck with the audience: they may want to leave at the interval, but if they stay on they must do so until the end, and transport will be arranged back to hotels.

For once, the actors have that cocoon of darkness they have missed in the opening scenes, and Hamlet's meeting with the Ghost strikes an appropriate note of terror. By the interval they're playing under a calm, starlit sky, and in the second half they achieve a thrilling and magical intensity. At the end Simon leads the company in applauding the audience. 'Normally I hate actors doing that, it looks so self-congratulatory,' he says afterwards. 'But this time I wanted to do it. I thought, Poor sods, it's half-past twelve, they deserve a medal for sticking in there.'

Friday 25 August

The actors leave Elsinore for Copenhagen, from where they will fly back to London. The trip is considered a success. The Danish notices have been excellent, calling Simon the finest Hamlet of his generation; the Swedish critics who have crossed the water to Elsinore have also been very approving. Despite the atrocious conditions there have been no cancellations, and the eight performances have been a sell-out.

'The trickier the weather, the more responsive the audiences have been,' Stephen says. 'Because they've invested so much, they've got an enormous payoff. The whole experience here has helped everyone bond together, so that we're now a very strong and happy company. Part of that is due to Simon, who insists that the production is about sixteen actors, and not just one. He doesn't play the star offstage, he's friendly with the crew and talks to everybody, and that engenders in the company a desire to do well.'

5.   *The London Opening*

Wednesday 30 August   The rehearsal room at the National. Morning. The actors have reassembled to prepare for this evening's performance, the first of five before next Tuesday's press night. It's six weeks since the previews were held in the Lyttelton, so this afternoon Trish and Stephen will top and tail the production technically, re-rehearse exits and entrances, and go through the lighting cues now that the full complement of chandeliers is restored to the set.

The morning is spent working in detail on several scenes or parts of scenes. A few clearly need attention after Elsinore; others have been causing concern in the previews. In some cases they have been identified by Stephen, in others by one or more of the actors. 'Today is about sorting out niggles and shaking Elsinore away,' Stephen says. 'The aim is to turn things that have been bellowed and big into something intimate and domestic again.'

One such is the opening scene, which he feels should be 'swifter and smaller'. Another is Hamlet's clifftop meeting with the Ghost. Stephen suggests to Sylvester that he could be less of a tormented spirit, and more of a father passing on a responsibility to his son. A third is Polonius' pastoral/comical speech, where Hamlet's and Rosencrantz and Guildernstern's laughter has been peaking too early.

Cathryn and Denis work a little on the scene in which Polonius forbids Ophelia to see Hamlet. They try to pinpoint more precisely when it turns serious; John had said earlier they were playing its outcome at the start. 'I have to try and lighten it,' Cathryn says. They play it, and she does so. 'That time I believed it,' Denis says.

In Elsinore Sara had been unhappy about having to play the closet scene in an exaggerated way, so she and Simon play it again, bringing it down a few notches. They feed off each other expertly, making small adjustments to their moves to give the argument a greater coherence.

The actors also look at Laertes' departure for France. Peter wants to put over more strongly the idea of a happy and relaxed court, one which only later starts to fall apart. Meanwhile both Guy and Simon have been concerned that until Hamlet's apology just before the duel, when he calls Laertes 'brother', there is no sign that the two know each other. It's agreed that a hint of this should be given in the scene. At first Guy tries touching Simon on the shoulder as he leaves; then a handshake is suggested. 'Make it a hard handshake,' Simon says. 'I need to boost my heterosexuality all I can.'

Afterwards Simon talks about the effect the Elsinore week has had on the production. 'Our performance had to be much grander, and also much simpler, otherwise it got swallowed up by the wind. The verse had to be more muscular, more banged out, which isn't a bad thing; the bounce does provide you with a kind of confidence. Making it more economical wasn't as difficult as I thought it would be, because the audience couldn't see the minutiae. But it was an odd experience, there were so many practical things to think of: making sure you were being heard, turning your face in the right direction.

'I'm sure when John comes back he'll have some strict words to say about all the original intentions that we've lost. That's why it's been good to have this morning's session, just to be able to get back to the words and think about them again. In the closet scene, for instance, the emotional landscape is still there, but what we'd lost was all the detailed thought.'

He is, he admits, longing to be back in the Lyttelton. 'Doing the play at Elsinore without the original set was a real trial of strength. I kept wanting to say to the audience, This is not the show you'll see in London – which of course would have been unfair. But I can't wait to get back to the original set, because it's such an integral part of the production, and it looks so ravishing and beautiful in the Lyttelton.'

Saturday 2 September

Evening. The stage management box at the back of the Lyttelton. With a clear view of the stage through a glass screen, Fiona Bardsley is seated at the controls, a board full of lights and switches. In her headphone set she has three separate 'rings': one connecting her with the sound and the musicians, another with the flies, stage management and stage crew, and a third with the lighting team.

Next to her is an infra-red monitor, allowing her to see what's happening on stage during any blackout: as the eyes and ears of the production she keeps a constant watch for problems or mistakes. She also controls the complex sequence of sound, music and lighting cues, of which there are about a hundred in *Hamlet*. 'You have to be able to concentrate and keep calm, and not panic if something goes wrong,' she says.

The performance begins. 'LX cue one, fly cue one, sound cue one – stand by.' In between giving the instructions Fiona talks through the headphones with Pete Bull on lighting and Adam Rudd on sound, who sit at computerised desks in control rooms on either side of her. Together they pinpoint any technical elements needing attention: a 'birdie' light at the front of the stage needs adjusting in one scene, to catch Simon's face better; the lighting in another seems to come up too gradually; the music linked to the opening of the back wall is a fraction too early. Fiona also talks frequently to Trish, Val and Andrew backstage.

Interval. The Lyttelton flytower, high above the stage. In an early scene the actors had been disturbed by noise from the flies, and Trish has come up to check on what happened with the man in charge. He and seven others are positioned on a narrow walkway, from where they operate by hand the numerous pulleys, cradles and counterweights that control the raising and lowering of the chandeliers.

The play resumes. Backstage, Trish sits in the prompt corner 'on the book', while also keeping a wary eye on her monitor on the flying of the chandeliers. Nearby Denis, now in his Gravedigger costume, is climbing into his 'grave' ready to be pushed on stage. 'I spend nine minutes in this bloody box,' he says in mock horror. 'You see how I suffer for my art?'

As the play continues Val and Andrew move around the wide spaces behind the side walls, where the various props, labelled in white to be visible in the semi-dark, are set out on long tables. Dressed in black costumes, they make sure the actors are in position at the right moment, occasionally joining them on stage for the more complicated scene-changes and box-shifting.

Trish deals with a few routine problems: an actor goes missing, but is found just in time for his cue; one of the musicians is heard practising on the recorder in a dressing-room, so Andrew is dispatched to stop the playing. Overall the performance is a smooth one technically, and her nightly report a very satisfactory one.

Tuesday 5 September

Press night. For Lucinda in the press office the unusual timetable has proved a blessing. Normally interviews with the company have to be arranged late on in the rehearsal period, when the actors and director have little time or energy to spare. 'Having the press night so late was an enormous advantage,' she says. 'Journalists have been able to come and see the show in the Lyttelton, and talk to Simon when he had some time off, or even in Malvern, before writing their pieces. Normally he gets quite nervous about interviews, but he's terribly willing. This time he'd done the previews, the show was up and running, and so he was more relaxed.' The result has been four extensive interview-based features before the official first night.

Few actors enjoy press nights, and Simon is no exception. 'I hate them, they're a real trial,' he says before the performance. 'I'm trying not to think about it too much. *Hamlet* will never get universal admiration, it's such an enormous piece. Some people won't be happy that we've cut all the Fortinbras stuff – although this far on I've forgotten that it's missing; the play as we're doing it seems to be quite coherent without all the geo-politics. Really I just want to get tonight over, and then I can sit back and enjoy the play.'

Before the performance John gives the actors the advice he gives every company he works with, recommending them not to read the reviews. If they have to do so, he asks them not to assume that anyone else in the company will want to know what they say. 'If you do read them, don't take them too seriously,' he says. 'The people to take seriously are your audiences, how they respond, what they feel and what they say. What matters is the relationship between you, them and the author.'

With the benefit of six previews and five ordinary performances in the Lyttelton, the actors come up with a fine ensemble performance that holds the audience throughout, and provokes a sustained ovation at its end. Simon very quickly sheds his nerves and is on top of his form. Beforehand he had placed a framed picture of his mother on the prop table. 'It meant so much to me,' he says afterwards. 'Every time I came off she was there.'

Thursday 7 September

The critics are almost unanimous in their praise of Simon's performance. Dismissing the notion that he might be physically unsuited for the role, they write admiringly of the intelligence, wit and moral authority of his Hamlet, and the crystal-clear and unaffected way he handles the verse. Rare, remarkable, haunting, perfect are among the epithets used. The other actors get a more mixed reception and, in many cases, totally conflicting comments on their performances.

The views on the production are also mixed. As Simon anticipated, many of the critics find fault with the decision to cut Fortinbras and the politics. They argue that the play is diminished if it is treated as a domestic, personal drama within Elsinore, and that the warrior Fortinbras is useful as a foil to Hamlet the thinker. John's production is seen as original and imaginative by some, but others dislike the overtly religious emphasis, reinforced by the motets and the cathedral-like set. There is also some uncertainty about his concept of the actors as ghosts, and a general dislike of the luggage-based scene-shifting.

Monday 11 September
The Sunday critics have come up with much the same range of views as those on the daily papers. While writing warmly of Simon's lucid and heartfelt Hamlet, their comments on the production are less ecstatic, with the absence of Fortinbras and the political backdrop again being widely mourned. Meanwhile, with several critics having crossed the Atlantic, some very appreciative reviews have begun to appear in the American press

John sticks to his policy of not reading the critics. 'They have an important job to do, but their relationship should be with the audience, not the creative artists,' he says. 'I find reviews disturb me whether they're positive or negative. I'm as disturbed by feelings of pride that my work is being appreciated as I am by feelings of disappointment if it isn't. I find both feelings irrelevant to my thought-processes, so increasingly I shut them out.'

Simon had originally decided to take John's advice. 'I told my family and friends and the cast I wasn't going to read the reviews, and they were all fine about it,' he says. 'But then Sara phoned me after the opening last week and said, I know you're not reading the notices, but I'm told they're good. So then I read them almost immediately; I decided not to be a puritan after all! I'm not sure whether the other actors are reading them or not. Nowadays you assume people don't, so out of courtesy you don't talk about it.

'My biggest relief was that my decision not to play Hamlet as mad came off. I knew that was a risk, and it was cowardice really, I didn't know where the madness would go, so I thought I'd have to take another route. But most critics seemed to get the idea of what we were trying to do. I was also pleased that the ones who liked it saw a romantic performance. That was entirely to do with John's faith, which I thought misguided, in seeing me as a romantic actor. He gave me tremendous confidence, encouraging me to be just who I am, and not worry about the way I look or move.'

After the wounding Malvern headline he seems relaxed about the constant references to his physique. 'In the end they really haven't worried me. I am the shape I am, and they haven't been offensive. One critic called me overweight, which pleased me, because it was so non-judgemental. If they'd said, He's grotesquely fat and therefore he cannot play this part, I would have been very upset.'

6. *The Tour Continues*

T wo weeks after the press night the company is due to resume the UK part of its tour. But before that a crucial event takes place in the Lyttelton: a full understudy performance, played to an audience of some fifty people scattered around the stalls, most of them friends of the actors.

Previous understudy rehearsals have been sporadic. Some work was done in Malvern, but none was possible in Denmark, and much of the time since returning to the National has been spent getting the production in as good a shape as possible. Before the performance Stephen explains: 'We had just three days last week, in effect fifteen hours, which isn't ideal for a production this size. Today will be useful for finding out which of the actors I still need to do more work with. But the performance will be especially important for Simon Day, who's put in a lot of work, and will now have the chance to play Hamlet at least once before an audience.'

He proves to be an impressive Hamlet. An excellent verse-speaker, he's a harsher, more intense and bitter prince than the other Simon. The other principals provide intriguing contrasts to the actors they're standing in for: Janet Spencer-Turner is a more fragile Gertrude, Chloe Angharad an angrier Ophelia, Martin Chamberlain a more ferocious Claudius. In the few places where two characters being understudied by the same actor appear on stage together, Stephen plays one of them with a script in his hand, a situation that inevitably poses an extra challenge to the actors.

Afterwards Simon Day ponders on the experience. 'It felt like a good showing. It certainly gave me a window on what Simon goes through every night. It's like getting on this enormous thoroughbred racehorse, which is a joy to ride, but gives you no time to think, Have I messed up that scene? because it just keeps going.

'I've watched Simon a lot, and tried to be as honest as I could about the part. I loved going on the stage and seeing what would happen, opening myself up to the experience. When you play Hamlet you bare your soul and your personality comes through. I was probably an angrier Hamlet than Simon, but also a less funny one. He gets a lot of laughs, and I think that it's tremendous to be able to do that in a tragedy. But I felt I didn't know how to get them without faking it.'

With the understudies firmly established in their roles, the actors take to the road again. During September they do a week each in Brighton and Glasgow, followed by a week at the Dublin Festival in early October. They then return for a further 24 performances in repertory in the Lyttelton before going abroad again in December for a week in Stockholm.

At each theatre the production is received with great enthusiasm. No audiences are more enthusiastic than those in the Stadsteatern in Stockholm, where the play is listened to with intense concentration, and the actors are called back for countless curtain calls during standing ovations. But some audiences are less attentive. At one performance at the Gaiety in Dublin the rowdy behaviour of school groups attracts dozens of complaints from the audience during the interval, and the management has to make an announcement over the tannoy before the second half can begin. But equally annoying is a mobile phone, which rings throughout Hamlet's 'What a piece of work is a man' speech.

In Glasgow there's a special school matinee at the Theatre Royal, with 1200 children booked in for the performance. Simon is terrified at the prospect, imagining that 'The last thing they want is an overweight, middle-aged Englishman talking to them about life and death.' Before the curtain rises the noise is intense, and bits of paper are flying across the auditorium. But once the play starts the children seem mesmerised, and at the end there are raucous cheers.

Like most actors, Simon has mixed feelings about an audience made up of school parties. 'I love kids coming to the theatre, because we need them, they're our future audience. But it can be very difficult playing to them, because many of them just don't want to be here. You just have to say to yourself, If there's one person who goes away inspired by what we're doing, then that makes it worthwhile.'

The critical reception on the tour is mostly very positive. The Irish press are particularly effusive, and in general more appreciative of the subtleties and visual beauty of the production than the English critics have been. In Scotland there is also enthusiasm, though one critic with a rather obvious nationalistic chip on his shoulder can't find a good word to say about this 'utterly E-N-G-L-I-S-H...stiff upper-lipped and most frigid of *Hamlets*'.

Each venue poses a different problem for the National's technical and stage management team. In the Theatre Royal in Brighton the chandeliers have to be flown using heavy hemp ropes. With no counterweights, this means having two men for each rope, so the cues have to be simplified. In Stockholm, by contrast, the theatre is equipped with a power fly system operated by one man at a computer. This allows for a more sophisticated lighting design than has been possible even in the Lyttelton, where a shortage of manpower on the flies has ruled out some of the original ideas.

After the unhappy compromise at Malvern, it was agreed that for the smaller theatres there would be a simpler, more coherent set, with uniform black flats, just a single entrance in the back wall, and a ceiling from which some of the chandeliers could be hung permanently. There has also been a return to one of the original ideas, of using the luggage to create parts of the walls. The result has satisfied everyone.

During the tour Trish continues to keeps a wary eye on the running time, which sometimes increases by three or four minutes. 'I have to tell the actors when they're slowing down, and that can drive them insane. One or two of them get so caught up and lost in the moment, they forget. I do feel a bit crass having to tick them off and get them to speed up. But they know that in watching the play every night I participate in the event and am therefore in a position to make a judgement.'

Throughout the tour Simon works to improve his performance. After the Stockholm week he is still unhappy about some of his speeches. 'The first soliloquy is going through a bad patch: I think the balance should be lighter, it's become a bit aggressive. The speech after the Ghost disappears has become a one-note rant, and I need to see how far I can take it down. The recorder speech doesn't work sometimes, I seem to get the rhythm wrong. And I can't seem to get enough different colours into the chapel scene, where I consider killing Claudius while he's at prayer.

'The one that's working quite well is "Oh what a rogue", I think because it's broken up into clearly defined sections, and because it's the one where I most directly address the audience. As for "To be or not to be", it's wonderful when it works, but that's quite rare. Although it's a stopping soliloquy, it musn't grind to a halt. It's a delicate balance, and I tend to slow down far too much. The sentences are oddly constructed, and you can lose the main verb. Also "puzzles the will" comes at a very odd place, and if you slow down too much before that on "the undiscovered country", you have a problem.

'On the positive side, the closet scene has become a completely moveable feast. I love it, because every night I have no idea where it's going to go. Sara and I trust each other, and if one of us makes a small decision at the start, it takes us into a completely different area. Sometimes for instance we don't touch at all, and sometimes I end up very angry. It can go in completely opposite directions. It's a lovely feeling.'

Hamlet has consistently attracted full houses during the tour, as well as being a complete sell-out at the National. Before the play returns for another spell in the Lyttelton, Simon and John look back with pleasure on their work.

Beforehand Simon had been sceptical of the claims by other actors who had played Hamlet that it could be a life-changing experience. Now he is not so sure. 'The part just adapts itself to you, it's one of the most hospitable an actor can play. It says, Come and get me, I've got everything here, just pick what you want. But it does demand that you strip everything away. Hamlet takes you right through that process, until you end up with nothing – "Let it be".

'As an actor the part enables you to say, I don't need to do any tricks, I don't need to show off in any way. You're able to stand on stage and allow people to have faith in you, to see that you are interesting as a human being – that of course applies to everyone on stage, but particularly to Hamlet. It's a most liberating experience, if you can get anywhere near that. You think, This is it, this is the Holy Grail of acting.'

For John, directing *Hamlet* has been a deeply rewarding experience. 'I've spent a great deal of my life wondering about Shakespeare. You get closer to him, then he recedes, then you get closer again; he's a wonderful mystery. But when you encounter him in the flesh through one of his great characters, then he is most emphatically present. There's nothing mysterious about him then, just a profound talent, which you're getting straight into the vein.

'*Hamlet* embodies those depths of thought and analysis and observation that Shakespeare was haunted by all his life, the dreams and uncertainties and inquiries about human existence that drove him. Those hauntings were what made him write three plays a year for fifteen years, and return constantly to those central characters who reflected his thoughts and visions about the way the world wags, whether it was Richard II, Rosalind, Cleopatra, Lear, Macbeth – or Hamlet.

'Always the greatest portrayers of those characters have been actors who have a Shakespearean imagination, which Simon certainly has. His greatness is contained within his rightness for the part. It's been an extraordinary privilege, and one that no scholar can have, however deeply they read the play: to get close to the man Shakespeare through a brilliant portrayal of his most profoundly philosophical character.

'I've seen many Hamlets, and admired some of them. But my only deep relationship with the play is one that I have developed in Simon's company. I think the way he has played Hamlet has taken me closer than I've ever been to understanding what Shakespeare is all about.'